Start TO Finish
Second Series

FROM Sugar Beet TO Sugar

LISA OWINGS

 LERNER PUBLICATIONS COMPANY ⟩ Minneapolis

Lerner Publications Company
A division of Lerner Publishing Group, Inc.
241 First Avenue North
Minneapolis, MN 55401 USA

For reading levels and more information, look up this title at www.lernerbooks.com.

Library of Congress Cataloging-in-Publication Data

Owings, Lisa, author.
    From sugar beet to sugar / by Lisa Owings.
        pages   cm. — (Start to finish, second series)
    Includes index.
    ISBN 978-1-4677-6020-1 (lib. bdg. : alk. paper)
    ISBN 978-1-4677-6290-8 (eBook)
    1. Beet sugar—Juvenile literature. 2. Sugar beet—Juvenile literature. 3. Sugar—Manufacture and refining—Juvenile literature. 4. Sugar trade—Juvenile literature. I. Title. II. Series: Start to finish (Minneapolis, Minn.). Second series.
TP390.O95 2015
664.123—dc23   2014016953

Manufactured in the United States of America
1 – CG – 12/31/14

TABLE OF Contents

Sugar is sweet! How is it made?

First, workers harvest the sugar beets.

White sugar is often made from sugar beets. Workers harvest sugar beets in the fall. Large machines pull the beets out of the ground and cut off the leaves.

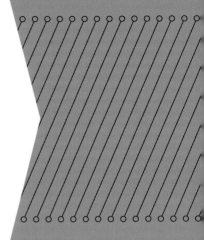

Then trucks carry the beets to a factory.

Loading machines shake off soil before piling the beets onto trucks. The trucks carry the beets to a factory and unload them on **conveyor belts**.

Next, the beets are washed.

The conveyor belts move the beets through a washing area. There, the beets are soaked in water to remove dirt and stones.

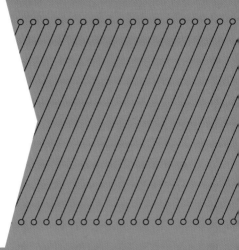

A machine slices the beets.

Next, the beets move to a slicing machine. The machine cuts the beets into thin strips. This **exposes** the beets' insides and makes it easier to draw out the sugar.

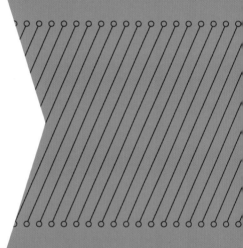

Then a machine extracts the sugar.

The conveyor belt feeds the sliced beets into a machine that extracts the sugar. The beets move upward as water flows downward. This releases the beets' sugar into the hot water.

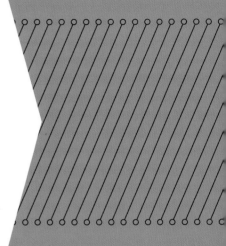

Next, workers purify the sugary liquid.

Workers mix chemicals into the sugary liquid. The chemicals form solids that trap unwanted substances. Next, workers filter out the solids to leave the liquid clean.

Then some of the sugar forms crystals.

Machines heat the liquid until some extra water **evaporates**. The remaining liquid turns into a thick syrup. Next, workers boil the sugary syrup and add **seed crystals**. White sugar crystals soon start to grow.

Crystals are separated from the liquid.

When the sugar crystals have grown large enough, workers move the mixture of crystals and syrup to another machine. This machine spins very fast. The force of its spinning separates the sugar crystals from the syrup.

Finally, the sugar is ready to eat.

The finished white sugar is washed, dried, and cooled. Machines pour it into bags. Then the sugar is sent to stores around the world. It's ready to become a sweet treat!

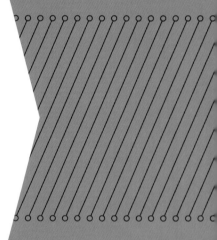

Glossary

conveyor belts: moving strips of material that carry objects from one place to another

crystals: solid substances with many flat surfaces

evaporates: changes from a liquid into a gas

exposes: reveals or shows something not first seen

extracts: removes something by pulling it out

harvest: to gather a resource for use

purify: to make something pure or clean by removing unwanted substances

seed crystals: small crystals from which larger crystals are grown

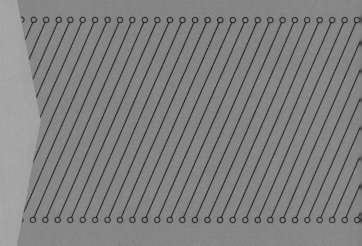

Further Information

Bence Reinke, Beth. *Sugars and Fats.* Mankato, MN: Child's World, 2013. Healthful eating is important. Check out this book to learn what role sugars and fats should play in your diet.

Boothroyd, Jennifer. *What Is Taste?* Minneapolis: Lerner Publications, 2010. Are your favorite snacks sweet, salty, or sour? Read this book to find out more about your sense of taste.

LaPenta, Marilyn. *Cool Cookies.* New York: Bearport Publishing, 2012. Ready to put your sugar to use? Try making some of the cookies in this recipe book.

Learning about Carbohydrates
http://kidshealth.org/kid/stay_healthy/food/carb.html#cat119
Check out this website for more information about sugars and other carbohydrates. Then click on some of the other healthful eating links.

Rock Candy
http://discoverykids.com/activities/rock-candy
Ask an adult to help you with this fun and tasty experiment. Watch sugar crystals grow into delicious rock candy!

Index

Photo Acknowledgments
The images in this book are used with the permission of:
© iStockphoto.com/Givaga, p. 1; © iStockphoto.com/
pkline, p. 3; © NHPA/Photoshot , p. 5; © Picture Alliance/
Photoshot , p. 7; AP Photo/Bernd Wuestneck/picture-
alliance/DPA, p. 9; REUTERS/photographer, p. 11;
© Avatar_023/Shutterstock.com, p. 13; AP Photo/Lee
Lockhart, Northern Wyoming Daily News, p. 15; © Hywit
Dimyadi/Dreamstime.com, p. 17; © Maximilian Stock Ltd /
Photo Researchers, p. 19; © Glen Stubbe/(Minneapolis Star
Tribune)/ZUMA Press, p. 21.

Front cover: © grafvision/iStock/Thinkstock.

Main body text set in Arta Std Book 20/26.
Typeface provided by International Typeface Corp.